EGG TEMPERA

Egg tempera is an ancient medium rarely used today. It is primarily composed of egg yolk, water, and dry pigments. It is water-soluble and dries very quickly to a permanent film. Its luminous appearance is what makes it unique. Many tempera paintings 500 to 700 years-old appear to be in better condition than the oils of the same eras. Egg tempera also makes an excellent underpainting for oil paintings, and many techniques can be employed with it. It is quite easy to use and, compared with other media, very inexpensive. The pigments are costly, but a little goes a long way. Moreover, panels, when handmade, cost much less than canvas, and the egg binder is far less expensive than any binder of which I am aware.

Few art schools teach egg tempera, and those that do generally offer it as some ancient and mystic craft practiced by icon painters. One needs only to view a collection of Andrew Wyeth paintings to begin to understand its potential. Cennino d'Andrea Cennini's *Libro dell' Arte* was for years the tempera painter's bible. Most of the available literature on egg tempera is filled with so many do's and don'ts that few would want to even try the medium. Take heart! In this book, the reader will discover how truly simple it is to paint with egg tempera.

I encourage you to select one or more of the demonstrations provided herein and experience the excitement of working with egg tempera. Whether you return to watercolor, oils, or acrylics afterward, it is my belief that you will return a better artist. If you never try painting with egg tempera, you will miss out on a great artistic experience.

CONTENTS

SUPPLIES

Pigments and Paints

You will need professional artist grade powdered pigment to use with the egg medium (see page 5). Since these pigments can be expensive, consider using good quality watercolors when practicing. China cups are excellent for mixing small quantities of paint, but once the tempera dries it cannot be used again.

Lidded plastic cups or baby food jars are the best choice for storing large quantities of paint. Most pastes without the egg medium in them will keep up to one week.

Brushes and Other Tools

Since egg tempera is a water-based paint, watercolor brushes work best with it. Bristle brushes make the best scumbling and dry brush tools. An old toothbrush can be used for splattering. A frisket knife and single-edge razor blades are best for scraping. Many varieties of sponges are available; start with a synthetic kitchen sponge, and purchase a greater variety later.

Miscellaneous Supplies

Butcher trays are arguably the best palettes, but plastic watercolor palettes can also be used. You will also need India ink and pens, plus 2H and 2B pencils. Finally, get two large cups, one for water and one to hold the egg yolk medium.

Surfaces

Many different surfaces can be used for painting with egg tempera. The one recommended most often is wood or hardboard coated with a paste made out of animal glue and gesso powder (both available in art supply stores). These panels are not difficult to make, but the process can be time-consuming. To mix the paste, add 15 parts water to 1 part animal hide glue, and then heat the mixture—don't boil! Once dissolved, take the clear glue mixture and spread it over the entire board to seal the pores and allow to dry overnight. Next, heat 5 parts animal glue and 3 parts gesso powder in a boiler, stirring until any lumps have dissolved. Then strain the mixture through muslin into a double boiler, and continue heating (do not boil!) for 30 minutes, until bubbles rise to the top. Finally, pour or brush the mixture onto the sealed panel and allow to set.

Ready-made gessoed panels are also available at most major art supply stores and have proven to be excellent for use with egg tempera. Watercolor board and illustration board are other good choices. When using paper, be sure it is 100% rag and acid-free. According to most of the manufacturers I have talked with, papers of this quality will probably outlast most canvases and panels. The artist's primary concern in choosing a surface should be to make sure that the board will not bend, causing the paint to crack, ruining the painting. Another option is to mount casein canvas onto a board; tempera works very well on this surface.

Important: Do not use acrylic gesso because tempera has difficulty adhering to its plastic surface.

Before you proceed with any of the projects in this book, read the instructions through first. Then mix up the colors with the medium ahead of time. You will get about four to six hours of painting time if you keep the paint in plastic or glass jars. You may wish to mix the colors to a paste and then add the egg medium as you go.

MIXING THE EGG MEDIUM

1. Take an egg and carefully separate the yolk from the white.

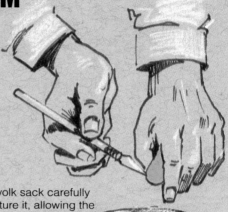

2. Hold the yolk sack carefully and puncture it, allowing the yolk to flow into a container; throw away the yolk sack.

3. To whatever volume of yolk you have, add an equal amount of distilled water.

4. Take professional grade pigment, place it in a lidded jar, and then add water until it makes a creamy paste.

Note: grinding may be required in order to crush the pigment.

5. Add the egg medium to the paste. Try to achieve equal amounts of paste and egg medium.

For convenience, egg and oil emulsion tempera is available in art supply stores. It consists of egg and linseed oil as its binder. It closely resembles traditional formulas and comes in a wide range of colors. It is water-soluble until dry.

Egg tempera was used prior to the first century AD, and there have been many formulae used over the centuries. Tempera is one of the easiest paints to make, it doesn't take very long to mix, and it is extremely economical. Good quality pigments are costly, but they are still not as expensive as oils. Because tempera is applied in very thin layers, it takes a long time to use up a jar of pigment. Eggs are the cheapest binder available, and the paint thins with water, so cleanup is easy with soap and water. You will find that egg tempera has a luminosity not found in other paints and a very distinctive appearance.

OTHER FORMULAE

Not all tempera painters use the formula listed on page 5. The tempera paint carried in most art supply stores contains linseed oil. This additive allows you to work on a wider variety of surfaces and to use slightly thicker applications of the paint. With linseed oil, you may have to wait a little longer for the paint film to dry before repeated glazes, but this should not be a major consideration.

You do not have to become a chemist to paint with egg tempera. I have included three other formulae below for those who like to experiment.

Formula I

1. Combine the following ingredients:
   1 whole egg (volume of egg = 1 part)
   1/2 part Damar varnish
   1/2 part linseed oil
   A = the collective volume = X
2. Add 1 or 2 drops of distilled water (stir, do not whip).
   Continue adding 4 or 5 drops of distilled water at a time and
   stirring until the amount of water (B) is equal to X.
   B = X
   A + B = C
   C = the collective volume = 2X
3. Add C to an equal amount of Damar varnish (D).
   D = 2X
   C + D = E
   E = the collective volume = 4X
   E = Egg Medium

Note: Many artists believe that adding egg white causes the paint to become brittle.

Formula II

1. Place 1 egg in a jar and stir.
2. Add an equal volume of Damar varnish (collective volume = A).
3. Add linseed oil equal to volume A (collective volume = B).
4. Add distilled water in an amount equal to volume B
   (B = C in volume).

Formula III

Mix the following ingredients:
25 to 40 grams gum Arabic in 35% solution
5 to 10 grams glycerin
1 egg yolk
2 grams commercial preserver

Note: This third formula, in essence, is simply egg yolk medium mixed with tube watercolors.

Now the modeling begins in earnest. Lay out four china dishes and fill with cadmium red light, viridian, flesh (yellow ochre, cadmium red, and white), and titanium white. (Ice cube trays can be used in lieu of china dishes.) Then using a fine-tipped watercolor brush, dip into the viridian green and begin crosshatching in the shaded area and the edges where the form turns. Continue building the form with cadmium red light and pink-flesh crosshatching. Finish with white highlights.

A more traditional approach would stop at this point, but a great amount of depth can be added with minimal glazing. Place a thin, transparent glaze (see page 17) of cool red over all the flesh areas. When dry, glaze the shadow areas with more viridian. Use a dark grey mixture of burnt sienna, ultramarine blue, and titanium white to accentuate the cloth.

Here is my version of *Mattias de Medici* by Justus Susterman. Although Susterman painted in oils, this reproduction was done completely with egg tempera. Every step used in the previous exercise was also employed here. This method of painting has a very distinctive look and is an excellent approach to portraiture. Again, it is time-consuming but worth the extra effort. **Note:** When signing work that has been copied from another artist, it is customary to acknowledge the original artist. The term "apre" simply means "after" and indicates that the painting is my version of a work done by another artist—in this case, Justus Susterman.

Charcoal drawing
on toned paper

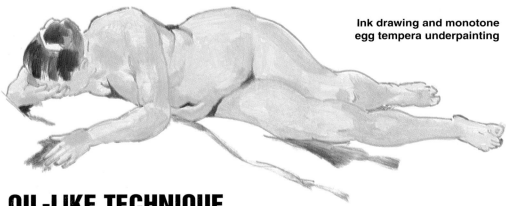

Ink drawing and monotone
egg tempera underpainting

OIL-LIKE TECHNIQUE

Some oil painters, such as Maxfield Parrish, used a monochrome underpainting with many layers of transparent color on top. This technique yields very luminous color, but it requires long pauses between the application of each layer to allow the paint to dry. Egg tempera can be used to accomplish a similar look, and each layer dries in just minutes. **Note:** This painting relies on glazing over a monotone egg tempera underpainting and does not include the crosshatching steps, yet it is still quite effective. This is the method used by fifteenth century artists such as Rogier Von Der Weyden. The only difference is that he put oil glazes on top of his tempera.

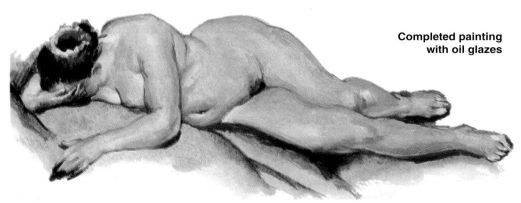

Completed painting
with oil glazes

MODERN TECHNIQUES

An example of "splattering" is shown to the right. This effect is created by loading a bristle brush or toothbrush with paint and running your finger across the bristles, spraying the surface with a splattering of paint. Simply change the angle of the brush to vary the shape of the splatters.

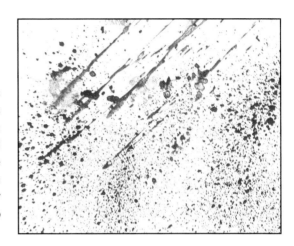

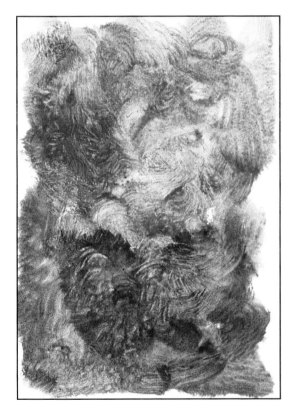

To the left is a technique called "scumbling." To create this effect, use a bristle brush loaded with paint and rub the bristles in circular and back-and-forth motions with either opaque or transparent color.

Note: One of the many reasons artists use tempera and other water-based mediums is the variety of techniques that can be employed.

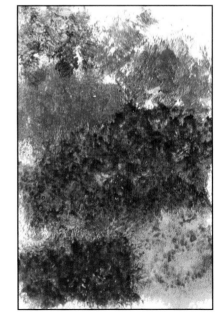

The effect to the right is known as "stippling." It is created by repeatedly applying the paint in a vertical motion. Bristle brushes work best for this technique.

Each of these effects is quite simple to master. Practice each one on scrap paper until you are satisfied with your results.

Achieving an opaque look without applying a lot of paint can be tricky. One approach is to load a soft sable brush with paint, turn it on its side, and tap it against the panel or board; this is called "tapping."

"Dry brush" is created by loading a brush (sable or bristle) with paint, wiping most of the paint off of the brush, and then dragging the brush across the surface. This technique is often used to simulate a wood grain effect.

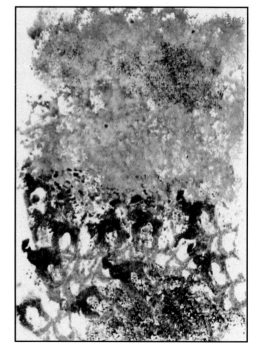

Sponges can be used to create many interesting effects in a painting. They come in a multitude of shapes, and each leaves a different imprint. Experiment with different types; synthetic sponges work best, but try some natural sponges for variety. Simply soak up some paint with the sponge and press it against the board. (**Tip:** This is an excellent technique for creating rock textures.)

GLAZING

Glazing is simply a transparent layering of color—that is, laying one thin layer of color over another. For instance, a glaze of blue over a glaze of yellow will appear green; this is because light pours through the transparent layers of color and reflects back as green. The whiter the base or background, the greater the reflection. (Note: Glazing is not unique to egg tempera; it can also be used with watercolor, oil, and other types of paint.)

You can use this technique to obtain richer, cleaner colors. Human skin, for example, is made up of layers. Beneath the pigmented outer layer of skin there are red muscle tissues and blue-green veins. Therefore, an underpainting of greens and reds followed by glazes of skin tones would create a more realistic illusion of depth.

Notice how light passes through layers of color and also reflects off the surface and other pigmented particles. One can glaze with almost any color, although some pigments are transparent while others are more opaque. Yellows and whites are far more difficult to make transparent, but, if thinned enough with medium, even these can be effective.

One old portrait painter's technique was to paint a head in grey or brown monotones and then glaze the shadow and lower areas (the chin and neck) with cool greens. In the areas farther up the face, such as the nose, cheeks, and ears, the glazes contained more red because in these areas the veins and blood vessels are closer to the surface. Then yellow was used for the forehead.

COMBINING TECHNIQUES

It is very helpful to experiment with small studies like these. For ease, mix some egg medium and combine it with watercolor. You will need a watercolor brush, a single-edge razor blade, a sponge, and a piece of illustration board or watercolor paper.

This example is from a demonstration I gave in Los Angeles.

The rock is created in four simple steps: (1) sponge in a light tone for texture; (2) use a toothbrush to splatter on a darker color; (3) create the reflected light by simply scraping the paint away with a frisket knife; (4) glaze the shaded areas with a cool, dark transparent color.

Create the wood fence by laying down a wash and then applying dry brush strokes over it. Dark blue-brown is used for the shadows and crevices. Use a single-edge razor blade to scrape off the paint for the highlights.

The wall is created by using a sponge technique over a wash. A blue-brown over-painting is used on the lower wall and the cracks. A razor blade is used again to scrape away the highlights. Scraping is a wonderful technique if not overused; take care to scrape only the paint; do not dig into the surface of the board.

MANY STYLES

Tempera can be applied in several ways. The example at top left is created with washes, like a traditional transparent watercolor. At top right, the painting is closer to an opaque watercolor. To the right, the paint is applied in *alla prima* strokes, which are thick and glossy looking. Below is an example of solid opaque shapes which delineate the forms.

There is no reason to change your style simply because you change to egg tempera. Use whatever techniques and style you prefer.

Old shacks and barns can be quite enjoyable to paint. Sketching outdoors can also be very rewarding. After making a detailed pencil sketch, it is helpful to also make one or more color studies. The painting below is a color study in transparent watercolors.

Use a 2H pencil to lightly draw the old barn and the fence posts on illustration board. The initial lay in is made with ultramarine blue, burnt sienna, and yellow ochre. Then the grass and trees are scumbled in. The darkest darks are burnt sienna and blue. If any areas become too thick, such as the trees to the left, scrape off the paint, and start again.

Any of the exercises in this book can be done on illustration board. After you have further developed your skills, you can move on to more expensive gessoed panels. Also, remember that instead of using powdered pigment, watercolor can be mixed with egg medium. This mixture will dry with a glossier sheen, but the handling will be the same.

In the previous steps, a thin coat of yellow ochre was placed over all the wood on the barn and the fence posts. Now glaze burnt umber over the yellow ochre. Also glaze ultramarine blue over the shadow area of the barn. Place a wash of burnt sienna over parts of the pale blue tin roof to simulate rust; this is even more effective if dry brush strokes are used. Try to give the trees a little more form without adding more detail; the background should not vie for attention.

On a watercolor palette, mix ultramarine blue and burnt sienna. These two colors combine to make a rich black and a multitude of grey values. First, place a wash of clear water over the sky. Then start at the top with dark greys, laying in successively lighter shades of grey as you approach the tree line. If the surface is wet, add a little extra water to the paint to allow it to bleed slightly. Then complete the painting by adding final details. More dark accents are placed on the barn and posts. In the example, a piece of paper was used to mask off the barn and some burnt sienna was splattered over the foreground. Finally, take Naples yellow or yellow ochre and white and paint in highlights with a fine-tipped watercolor brush.

Painting Eagle Rock

While sketching in Laguna Canyon, California, I came across this interesting rock, which I named "Eagle Rock." A detailed rendering is the priority at this stage so that further detail and color can be applied later. The first step is to trace the outline on vellum and then transfer it to a board or panel. Cover the back of the vellum with ordinary colored chalk, and redraw the outline. Press down hard enough with a 2H pencil so the lines will transfer but not so hard that you create indentions in the board or panel.

There is a lot of green in this landscape. To give the color life, first lay in a thin wash of red, and then apply the green over it. Since red is the direct complement of green, the two colors will contrast, bringing more vibrance to the painting.

Both light and dark greens are added. The paint is applied in thin layers with a scumbling action. Do not be overly concerned about losing edges since they can be scratched out later. Place a pink wash over the rock and lay in a blue-brown middle tone. Also, add a few dark accents in the deep crevices.

The splatter technique was used to add texture to the rock. To isolate the rock and protect the background, trace the rock on a piece of bond paper, cut the shape out with a frisket knife, and then tape the mask over the image with drafting tape. The mask (shown above) will leave only the rock exposed. Then using a bristle brush or toothbrush, load the brush with paint and run a finger across it, spraying the rock with a spattering of paint. Repeat as often as necessary; then remove the mask.

As shown below, scrape off any unwanted splatters, and add some dark cracks and crevices as desired. Scratch out the highlights or use very light colored paint to add highlights.

Painting grass is very simple. Lay in a thin wash of yellow ochre over the entire area; then take the yellow ochre and darken it with burnt sienna. With a fine sable brush, make several vertical strokes. Then add some twigs with pure burnt sienna. Use yellow ochre and white to add some light accents.

Before you proceed with any of the projects in this book, read the instructions through first. Then mix up the colors with the medium ahead of time. You will get about four to six hours of painting time if you keep the paint in plastic or glass jars. You may wish to mix the colors to a paste and then add the egg medium as you go.

THE IMPORTANCE OF PEN AND INK

Drawing is a skill developed through practice. The more you draw, the better you get. It doesn't matter what subject you choose—just draw! Becoming skilled at pen and ink is important to the tempera painter because ink is often used as an underpainting with tempera. Always use India ink because it is permanent and readily accepts tempera. To further exploit this painting medium, you should become proficient at the use of line and crosshatching. These pages contain both coquille and technical pen drawings which can each be used as an underpainting. It is not necessary to use a fixative; simply apply the paint directly over the ink drawing.

PAINTING AN OWL

Birds of prey are interesting subjects to paint. First make a detailed ink or pencil drawing, and then trace the drawing and make any corrections on the tracing. Transfer the drawing to illustration or watercolor board. The primary goal at this stage is to establish the darkest area and half-tones. Mix raw umber and egg medium and scrubble lightly. The eyes, claws, and beak are brought to a near final state with black.

This painting has a warm palette. The colors used are cadmium orange, Hooker's green, ivory black, burnt sienna, ultramarine blue, raw sienna, and titanium white.

Cadmium orange and Hooker's green are used to create the nondescript background. The orange is used in the background to set off the orange eyes. The green is used in glazes to tone down the orange where it might detract from the main subject. Raw sienna is used in a thin glaze to cover the entire bird. Ultramarine blue and burnt sienna are used to delineate the tree.

Notice how detail begins to appear in this step. Raw umber is applied using horizontal strokes to indicate the breast feathers. Vertical lines and some crosshatching are used to develop the form around the head. Pure titanium white is applied in linear strokes over the raw umber, indicating the feathers on the chin and feet. Some white is also applied to the breast.

Notice that the tree limb now has great depth. More dark bark is added, and the highlights are created by scratching out paint with a frisket knife. The wood is then covered with a glaze of Hooker's green. Glazes of green, blue, and burnt sienna are used to add depth and finish the form of the owl.

PAINTING TREES

Here are two sketches of trees: one is a rough pencil composition, the other a detailed ink drawing. Both are excellent reference materials.

Use pencil to lay out your composition. Make certain that you are happy with it before continuing. Once satisfied, transfer the drawing to your painting surface. **Note:** before you begin painting, you may want to do a few small color studies to establish the mood—for example, the following demonstration has a mysterious sky.

Once the composition is laid out in pencil, a wash of alizarin crimson and ultramarine blue is placed in the sky, as shown on the opposite page. To give the trees life, a thin wash of cadmium yellow is laid over them.

The trees are then painted with ultramarine blue, Hooker's green, burnt umber, and raw sienna. The nearest tree is scumbled with raw sienna first. The next tree is a mixture of raw sienna and Hooker's green. The third tree is a combination of ultramarine blue and burnt umber. Use some of this mixture to paint shadows on the near tree and dark accents on the others.

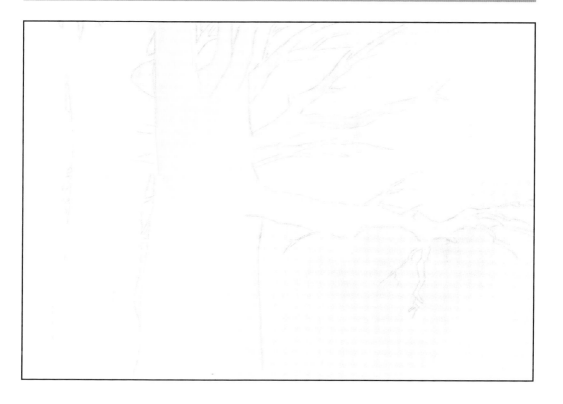

At this stage, the two back trees begin to get darker and cooler. Transparent layers of ultramarine and burnt umber are applied thinly until the desired result is achieved. Much detail is also added. The dark blue mixture is used to create the shadows of the bark. The light limbs and highlights are achieved by scraping off paint with a frisket knife.

The finished look here is created with more transparent glazes. To make an area recede, cool it with blue; to make it come forward, warm it with raw sienna. Always apply a light warm glaze over the scratched area so that the technique is not noticeable. The fine line branches are created by dragging a script liner brush away and up from the surface.

PAINTING A STREET SCENE

The illustration above is a simple watercolor sketch. The colors are the same as observed on location, but they change in the final painting. The point of interest is the doorway. To the right are some rough sketches of pigeons to be used in the final version.

A full pencil rendering is shown on page 39. This establishes all the dark and light values. These studies give the artist enough information to return to the studio and create an interesting painting. To paint this scene, you will need an illustration board, a frisket knife, a sponge, assorted watercolor brushes, and the following colors: raw umber, ultramarine blue, burnt umber, Hooker's green, cadmium red light, cadmium yellow, and white.

Make a pencil sketch of the scene above or simply make an outline on illustration board with a 2B pencil. As below, place a wash of raw sienna on the door. Establish the middle tones of the steps with a mixture of raw umber and blue. Scumble this on with a bristle brush. Make a darker mixture of the same colors and render the darkest shadows with a small watercolor brush.

Using cadmium yellow and white with a touch of raw umber, place a thin wash over the top section of the walls, the steps, and the sidewalk. Burnt umber is applied to the lower wall with a sponge. With a burnt umber and blue mixture, make dry brush strokes (see page 16) on the door to simulate wood. Lay out newspaper around the door, and splatter the door lightly with a toothbrush filled with burnt umber. Continue to darken the wall and shadow areas with Hooker's green and raw umber; this allows the colors to darken without becoming flat.

This is an exercise in wood, stone, and plaster. The pigeons are painted in opaquely; they add interest to the composition.

Apply another coat of burnt umber over the doorway. A dirty white is scumbled over the upper wall to lighten it. Then simulate age using the dry brush technique and raw umber. At this point, the doorway should appear solid.

Now add the "magic": the shadows are on the left, and the highlights are on the right. Take a frisket knife and lightly scrape away the paint to expose the lights. Do the opposite on the worm holes, scraping the left sides. Continue glazing and scraping until satisfied.

These barrel studies were made as references for background use in a cowboy painting I rendered several years ago.

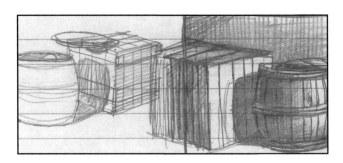

Although these were done for a specific reason, the barrel makes a good, simple object to use when experimenting. If you do not want to draw a barrel, take any simple prop, make a few sketches in pencil or charcoal, and then trace or resketch it on illustration board with a 2H pencil.

This barrel was painted with only three tempera colors: ultramarine blue, burnt sienna, and yellow ochre. It is not necessary to make up large quantities or many colors to do practice studies.

Don't get bogged down with too many elements when the idea is a simple learning sketch.

OIL OVER TEMPERA

This is an oil painting, but, unlike a regular oil painting, it was begun and brought to a more complete state with egg tempera. Because of the quick drying nature and ability to execute detail easily, tempera is an exceptional medium for underpainting.

The tempera underpainting was completed with ultramarine blue, burnt sienna, and yellow ochre. The highlights were then scraped out with a razor blade. A mixture of burnt sienna and sap green oil color was thinned and glazed over the entire picture. The surface is a gessoed panel; oil should never be used on paper unless the paper has been sealed to prevent it from deteriorating. When you paint the same subject over and over using different techniques, you can compare methods and decide which ones you prefer.

OIL OVER TEMPERA: PORTRAIT

Painting oil over tempera dates back to the fifteenth century. Most art historians claim that as oil paint became more popular, tempera was abandoned completely. It is quite interesting to note that one of America's great illustrators, Dean Cornwell, used this method on many of his paintings.

Having experimented first with the barrel, the next step is to use the technique on a serious subject. This portrait of noted California artist Michael Ward provides the perfect opportunity.

The first step is to make a comprehensive India ink drawing on panel. The tempera is used only to establish local colors and values. The underpainting is transparent and contains no white; it serves only to establish the design so that when the oil is applied there is no guess work. Ultramarine blue is used for the shirt, cerulean blue for the jeans. Flesh colors are jaune brilliant and cadmium red light. The background consists of washes of burnt umber and burnt sienna.

The final step is to apply the oil paint in thin layers. If desired, more oil in thicker layers can be added until totally satisfied. The real advantage here is speed. The egg tempera allows you to have a completely dry underpainting in one sitting.

ACRYLIC AS EGG TEMPERA

The egg yolk binder can also be used with acrylic paints. The binder takes some of the plastic look out of the acrylics. When one adds a plastic binder to tempera, however, the scratching out techniques are no longer possible.

The Process

A blue-green underpainting is first painted with an acrylic jar color and egg yolk medium at a 60% acrylic to 40% medium ratio. The egg yolk makes the acrylic dry even faster. Glazes of cadmium red and viridian green are used for the dark areas, and cadmium red light is used for the lighter side. Small amounts of cadmium yellow medium and cadmium red light are used for the stem, and white is added last for the highlights.

Note: For best results, try using acrylic gouache. The gouache is more versatile than ordinary acrylics, and it can be used with almost any technique.

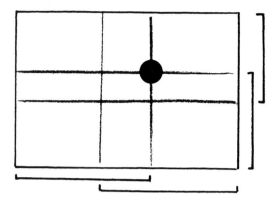

COMPOSITION

There are many theories regarding composition. Numerous books are devoted to the subject, and any serious artist should read one or more of them. (See Walter Foster book #194, *Composition Made Easy* by William Palluth.)

Once you determine what subject matter to paint, how you arrange the elements will have a major impact on whether the painting is a success or failure. The goal is to arrange the elements in such a way as to make the viewer look at it. Having looked, will that viewer look closely enough to see what you have communicated? And, with hope, enjoy the view? This may be overly simplistic, but if you cannot command an audience to notice your painting, then there will never be a response—good or bad.

The academic approach to composition is to employ the use of the "golden mean" or "golden section." This is a method of dividing a rectangle in such a way as to mathematically determine the best area to place the center of interest. The formula I was taught in art school is to measure each side of the panel or canvas and multiply each by .6, to find the 60% points (see illustration above left). Draw vertical and horizontal lines indicating the 60% points; the intersections determine the four areas on which to place the most important object or objects of the composition.

The illustration above right demonstrates how this is achieved; it clearly shows where to place the white cottage for the best effect. This example is an oil on egg tempera landscape.

There are, of course, other compositional approaches worth considering. The example to the left is an example of an "S" curve. The eye has no choice but to follow the "snake" to its destination.

The diagram to the right is an example of dominate mass. The object fills up the space and is the only thing at which to look. If it is in a triangle shape, it is also very

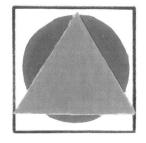

stable. If the triangle is turned upside down, however, it will create action.

Directors in the theater are very familiar with the use of spotlights. Above is an example of a very dramatic use of light—highlighting only the main element. This is called "chiaroscuro."

The head study above is also a dominate mass. Sometimes it can be effective to shift the subject slightly off-center.

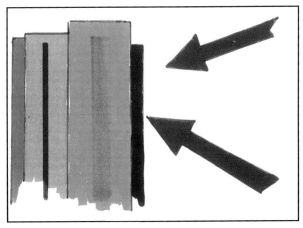

Another approach is to crowd the plane to one side. The dull negative space will send the eye searching for something to explore. An excellent example of this can be found on page 37 (trees).

My original idea was to trim this down and use it as a gallery page; instead, I decided it would serve as a good example in composition. The technique used is transparent watercolor and egg medium. It became apparent that the landscape overpowered the girl. I used a model friend and placed her in a background from a watercolor done many years ago; it simply did not wash. When cropped, as shown, it makes a decent painting. Remembering the principle of the golden section (see page 46) instructs me to leave the figure in the strongest area for maximum attention.

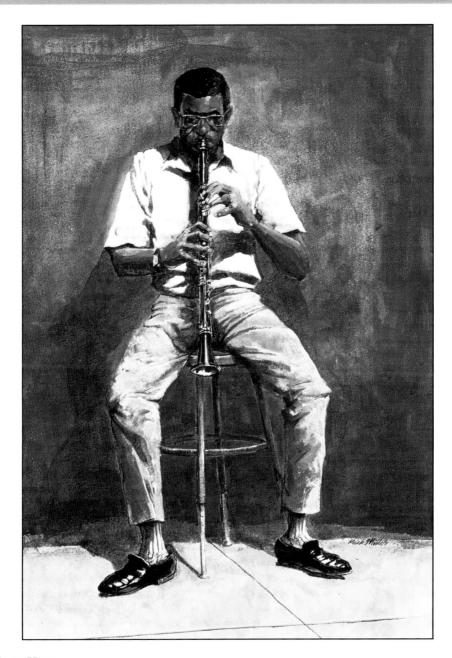

Jazz Man

This is a very simple composition: a dominant mass in the shape of a triangle. The cracks between the cement slabs are placed off-center to prevent monotony. Black is used on the shoes, on the horn, and in the hair. To prevent these areas from becoming flat, mix the black with deep purple and sap green. The skin tones are created with viridian green, burnt sienna, cadmium red light, and raw sienna.

RABBITS: A LINEAR LOOK

A linear ink style with some crosshatching creates an interesting composition. This particular painting approach attempts to capture a similar feel in egg tempera, as is evident in the line drawing above. The method used here is fairly straight forward. Begin with an ink drawing executed with an extremely fine ink pen. Note that the lines are drawn in the direction the fur is growing. This helps delineate the form as well as imply fur-like texture. This will be your major piece of reference.

After lightly drawing the sketch with pencil, lay in thin washes of color to tone the surface, eliminating the white paper. The background is a mixture of cerulean blue, raw sienna, and white. A combination of ultramarine blue, burnt sienna, and white is used for the grey undertone of the rabbits. Ultramarine blue and burnt sienna make the black for the eyes and noses. Cadmium green is used for the grass, thinned burnt sienna for the dirt.

Notice that the opaque paint is applied over the undertones in the same manner used in the ink drawing. A script brush works best for this because of its ease and ability to produce such delicate lines. In the dark fur areas, use a mixture of viridian green and burnt sienna. Straight burnt sienna is used in the rabbits' foreheads. The lighter areas of fur are painted with raw sienna, cadmium orange, and white. Finally, add small highlights to the eyes, ears, and nose areas with titanium white.

FLOWERS: OIL-EGG EMULSION

Whenever you paint a very busy scene, such as a basket of fruit, floral arrangements, crowd scenes, etc., it is best to make a comprehensive drawing to establish the patterns of dark and light shapes. The silhouette defines the object, but the values (shades of grey) give the object depth. One can stray from the drawing if desired, but if the drawing holds together well, the painting will probably look much better.

These flower studies were made in an attempt to become familiar with the separate elements. On a scrap piece of watercolor paper, try out a number of different brush strokes or color combinations to see if the effects will be pleasing. Have you ever seen an orchestra begin a concert without warming up? The same principle applies to painting.

This painting is begun with thin washes of egg tempera over the entire surface of the watercolor paper. Viridian green, cobalt blue, and some magenta is mixed with white and laid in randomly, as with a transparent watercolor. Only a hint of definition to the table edge is implied, and a slight shadow to the vase is suggested.

The vase and flowers are painted as if you are using opaque watercolor. Viridian green, cadmium green, and ultramarine blue are used for the flower stalks and leaves. Cadmium red deep, cadmium red, cadmium orange, cadmium yellow medium, lemon yellow, and white make up the palette for most of the flowers. A little magenta and ultramarine blue are used and combined to make the various crimson and purple flowers. The reason the colors are so bright is simple. A red flower, for instance, is painted cadmium red medium. Cadmium red deep is applied in the shadows. A touch of white mixed with cadmium red medium is then applied to the lighter side of the flower. The colors are not muddy because there is almost no mixed color, just pure color directly from the tube or jar.

Photo-realism, or magic-realism, was very popular in the nineteenth century, when painting still lifes with minute, lifelike details became a passion for many artists. Many artists today employ egg tempera to capture sharp focus painting because of the ease with which it can be used to delineate virtually microscopic detail. Both of these paintings were executed with small daubs of color and very tiny lines placed side by side or overlapping. Number 0 and 00 watercolor brushes were used for the minute strokes.

INK UNDERPAINTING

The unique feature in this example is the ink underpainting. The goal is to create a concrete or stone effect for the water fountain. This is achieved very simply by using India ink. The ink is dry brushed on the wall and textured with a sponge. Very thin washes of ink are then applied. When satisfied with the value and texture, glazes of raw umber, yellow ochre, and sap green tempera are added.

This is very similar to the watercolor washes over ink used by many children's book illustrators. The ink drawing leaves a grey and white monotone underpainting. All the colors are then applied with egg tempera, either in thin glazes or very opaque colors, such as in the girl's face, arms, and dress. Each area has one or more layers of color on it. One would not be able to do this with watercolor washes because the subsequent layers of color would affect the layers beneath.

In regard to technique, the parts are more interesting than the whole. Note first the clapboards and the door on which the middle tone is scumbled. This is followed by the grain which is drawn in, creating the texture. To become exceptionally talented at achieving detail, you must study textures, such as wood grain, tree bark, and fur. This is not a process that can be rushed; take your time, and put in as much detail as is necessary and pleasing.

The top of the doorway is not dark in the beginning. It is initially painted in the same value as the section above, then dark shadows are added by glazing with a mixture of blue-green and burnt umber. Sometimes two or three layers are applied.

Sometimes you will experience a "happy accident." Here some paint was inadvertently scraped off the siding slats; it looked interesting, so it was left alone.

Bricks are painted in with several shades of red and red-oranges. If they are too bright, simply glaze some green over them to cool or tone them down. A creamy white mixture is then applied for the cement. A few more dark accents are then added, as well as a shadow.

There is a lot of brown in this painting; burnt umber, burnt sienna, and yellow ochre are used extensively. These colors, like black, can be very dull. To avoid this, use the browns in the beginning for local color and underpainting. Establish the details first; then use sap, Hooker's, or viridian green in thin glazes over the browns. This technique is very effective in bringing life to dull colors.

GALLERY

The young man waiting for the fireworks is the main figure. Much more detail is used on him than on the other figures; he is also the highest in value.

The woman serving food is part of the composition, but if she or any of the others "pop out" too much, they will detract from the main figure

Paint background characters with the same detail and color as foreground characters. Then glaze over them—sometimes with many layers—until they begin to darken and fade. The highlighted white enamel pot is a compositional element that is used to guide the viewer's eye to the center of interest. The pot is extremely realistic. The colors used are cobalt blue and white. Add India ink to the blue for the top rim and handle. Pure titanium white highlights are added to make it shine.

If these characters were composed in a straight line, as they originally appeared, they would guide the viewer's eye off the page. To prevent this, the characters are rearranged to bring the viewer's eye back to the action.

In the painting to the right, notice that there is a great deal of dark space above the main characters. The eye goes immediately to the central character because he is wearing so much white. Also, the dark green column leads the eye to the man on the right and then back to the main figure.

This painting is created with a simple palette. The colors used are alizarin crimson, cadmium red light, burnt sienna, viridian green, sap green, ultramarine blue, cadmium yellow medium, yellow ochre, and titanium white. The flesh tones are created with mixtures of viridian green, cadmium red light, yellow ochre, and white. The terra-cotta pots are cadmium red light and burnt sienna; sap green and yellow ochre are the main colors in the column. All of the dark shadow tones are made with ultramarine blue and burnt sienna.

Chinese Sword Dancer is primarily a study in blue and red. The blues are a rich turquoise color. To create turquoise, mix viridian green and cerulean blue with white. Cadmium red and white make up most of the pinks. The dark pinks are made by adding viridian to the reds. The blues are darkened with ultramarine blue.

Oil glazes are always superior to egg tempera glazes. Particles suspended in oil will always reflect more light than particles suspended in egg yolk. Egg tempera is opaque, but transparent watercolor is not. I often paint an illustration or portrait in traditional egg tempera but then glaze with watercolors mixed with egg yolk medium. This mixture appears very similar to an oil painting. The headdress, the pearls, and the turquoise breast plate were all glazed with watercolor. This creates a glossy sheen which I then continue through the entire painting to make it consistent.

These little Alabama farm house paintings were my first egg temperas. Each was painted on location and then touched up in the studio.

The medium used was egg-tempera, but the paste was from tubes of transparent watercolor paint rather than powdered pigment and water. The paints were mixed as needed and thinned with water. The painting to the left was executed on a water-color block so it would not buckle; the painting below was done on a stretched casein canvas. (Today, one might chose a commercially manufactured gessoed board.)

A limited palette was used for both paintings: burnt sienna, ultramarine blue, cadmium red light, yellow ochre, sap green, and titanium white. **Tip**: When painting on location, try to keep things simple.

CARTOONING ANYONE?

You might never have thought of egg tempera as a suitable medium for cartooning or other humorous illustration—but think again! Pen and ink, gouache, and watercolor are the media that are most commonly used for cartooning; but with egg tempera's glazing and quick drying properties—plus all the techniques described previously—cartooning and caricatures can be even more expressive.

FIRST PUBLISHED EGG TEMPERA

When I painted this picture, I was a very serious oil painter. Woodi Ishmael, the famous illustrator and portrait painter, worked and taught in oil. Consequently, as one of his students, I followed suit. Early on, it became apparent that glazing techniques in oil would present a major obstacle to meeting magazine deadlines. Glazing with tempera, however, allows for the application of multiple layers within a single painting session. It is amazing that tempera is not more popular with today's professional illustrators.

Reprinted courtesy of Troy State University

CONCLUSION

This book, unlike many others, suggests that egg tempera is easy to use. It also suggests that panels currently manufactured are equal, or even superior, to most handmade panels. After many conversations with various paper manufacturers, I believe that 100% rag, acid free boards will, with care, outlast most painting surfaces. One of Italy's greatest tempera artists, Pietro Annigoni, states that he uses a silk rice paper mounted on canvas and then mounted on wood with fish glue. Some other famous egg tempera artists use gesso on hard board (masonite). We know that the paint formulae described earlier have been used for hundreds of years. Overall there is substantial evidence to support the claim that using these methods will result in paintings that last for hundreds of years.

There are, however, a couple of problems with egg tempera that should not be overlooked. If the paint is applied too thickly it might crack and fall off the surface. Another problem is known as "blooming." This is when a painting grows mold—some believe due to humidity. This should not be a major concern; It has only happened to me once with some paintings that had been stored in a closet for several years. Acetic acid or ordinary vinegar and cotton swabs remove the mold quite easily.

I rarely varnish my paintings. I have used an acrylic varnish without any problem but do not recommend it. Some manufacturers recommend using wax varnish. The painting can then be polished with a silk cloth.

To clean tempera, first dust the surface. If it is very dirty, rub lightly with cheese cloth, mild soap, and warm water. Tempera paintings have historically outlasted oils, the colors remain true, and, after they chemically dry, they develop a very tough skin. There is no stage, however, when they are immune to scratching. Take great care when stacking and transporting.

All painting media have some negative characteristics. On the whole, the advantages of egg tempera far outweigh its faults. It is extremely inexpensive to use and allows great flexibility. It becomes a simple matter of discovering what is unique about this medium and how best to exploit it. I hope I have been helpful in this regard. Please write and tell me of your successes!